WHAT · DO · WE · KNOW ABOUT THE AMAZONIAN INDIANS ?

ANNA LEWINGTON

SIMON & SCHUSTER
YOUNG BOOKS

First published in 1993 by
Simon & Schuster Young Books

© 1993 Simon & Schuster Young Books

Simon & Schuster Young Books
Campus 400
Maylands Avenue
Hemel Hempstead
Herts
HP2 7EZ

Design: David West
          Children's Book Design

Illustrator: Ian Thompson

Commissioning editor: Debbie Fox

Copy editor: Jayne Booth

Photograph acknowledgements:
Front and back cover: Magnum (Rio Branco); Sue
Cunningham/Sue Cunnningham Photographic: pp 9(b), 14, 15(tr),
15(b), 16, 18, 19(b), 22, 29(r), 30, 33(tr), 37(t), 38, 39(t), 40,
40–41, 42(l & r), 43(b); Mary Evans Picture Library: pp 39(b),
41(t); Fotograma/Rosa Gauditano (Granata Press Service): pp
23(cl), 41(b); Robert Harding Picture Library: pp 23(b), 34(t),
35(b) (Handbury-Tenison), 21(b); Dr Philip Hugh-Jones: pp
34(b), 35(t); The Hutchison Library: pp 12 and 24(b) John Wright
21(t) (Granada TV), 25(t), 29(l) (Brian Moser); The Hutchison
Library/W. Jesco von Puttkamer: pp 13(b), 25(b), 27(cr), 32–33,
33(b), 36; Impacr Photos: pp 31(t) (Ana C. Gonzales); Magnum:
pp. 21(c) and 24–25 (Rio Branco), 27(b) (C.S. Perkins); Jeffrey L.
Rotman Photography: pp 26; Edward Parker: endpapers and pp
9(tl), 9(tr), 15(tl), 17(t), 19(t), 20(l & r), 23(cr), 27(cl), 32, 33(tl),
36–37, 43(t); South American Pictures: pp 13(c) and 15(c) (Bill
Leimbach), 17(br) (Editora Index), 23(t) (Kimball Morrison);
South American Pictures/Tony Morrison: pp 28, 31(b), 37(b);
Survival International: pp 13(t) (Peter Frey), 17(bl) and 27(t)
(Stephen Corry); WWF Photo Library: p 35(c) (Y.J. Rey-Millet).

Picture research: Val Mulcahy

Printed and bound : by Paramount Printing, Hong Kong

A CIP catalogue record for this book is available
from the British Library

ISBN 0 7500 1322 2

Endpapers: Aerial shot of tropical rainforest in the state of Acre
in Western Brazil

· CONTENTS ·

WHO·ARE ·THE· AMAZONIAN INDIANS?

The Amazonian Indians have been living in the Amazon rainforest of South America for thousands of years. Today, about one million Indians are divided into around 500 different tribes. Each tribe has its own language, beliefs and customs, but all share basic ideas about the way they live. Indians believe that they share the forest with the animals and plants. When Europeans arrived in South America up to twelve or fifteen million Indians lived in Amazonia. Since then millions have died from Western diseases or cruel treatment. Amazonian Indians are still struggling to keep their lands and culture today.

INDIAN MIGRATION
The Amazonian Indians are thought to have migrated from Asia to South America about 10,000 years ago, via the Bering Straits.

Bering Straits

North America

Europe

Asia

Africa

South America

Australasia

Rainforest ▢

INDIAN LANDS
The Amazon basin covers an area of around six million square kilometres. This vast region, bigger than the USA, is made up of large stretches of open grassland as well as immense areas of tropical rainforest. It extends into nine different countries: Brazil, Peru, Ecuador, Colombia, Bolivia, Venezuela, French Guiana, Guyana and Surinam. As you can see from the map on the left, most of the rainforest lies in Brazil. The largest tribe of Indians, the Yanomami, are split between Brazil and Venezuela, with roughly 10,000 on each side.

Guyana
Venezuela
Colombia   10
            6
9   Surinam   8 French 4
Ecuador   Guiana
            1   2
Peru   Brazil
        3   7
                    5
        Bolivia

Chile   Paraguay

        Rio de
        Janeiro

        Uruguay

    Argentina

KEY
1. Aguaruna
2. Kayapo
3. Machiguenga
4. Marajo
5. Mehinaku
6. Tukano
7. Uru-Eu-Wau-Wau
8. Waimiri-Atroari
9. Waorani
10. Yanomami

SOUTH AMERICA

INDIAN POTTERY
Many Indian groups used to make pottery. Because of the humid climate, remains of pots are hard to find. The pot below was made by the Marajo people.

THE KAYAPO
The youth below is a Kayapo warrior. There are about 3,500 Kayapo who live in fourteen main villages north and south of the Xingu river in Brazil.

FOREST CONSERVATIONISTS
The Amazonian Indians know their environment very well. Over the centuries they have developed ways of growing what they need without destroying the forest permanently.

 MARAJO ISLAND

Most of the Amazonian Indian tribes that exist today are relatively small. There may be less than a few dozen people. But before the European conquest many tribes were enormous. One of the best known was located on the island of Marajo at the mouth of the Amazon. Archaeological evidence in the form of household remains and beautiful multicoloured pottery has been found there. The evidence suggests that the population of Marajo was at least 100,000. Marajo culture is known to have flourished for more than 1,000 years but mysteriously disappeared sometime before AD1300.

TIMELINE

	30,000-15,000 BC	AD 300-1300	1450-1550	1700-1800	1850-1914	
EVENTS IN THE AMAZON	By 15,000 BC people have already settled in the Amazon Basin having migrated south from what is now North America.	At least 100,000 people live on Marajo Island at the mouth of the Amazon between AD 300-1300. Their society is very complex and well organised and develops advanced pottery techniques.	Christopher Columbus arrives in the Caribbean and claims New World for the King of Spain in 1492. In 1493, Pope Alexander VI divides the lands between Spain and Portugal.	In 1742, Juan Santos Atahualpa brings together the Yanesha and Ashaninka peoples of Peru to resist colonial invasion of their rainforest territory.	'Rubber boom' in Amazon 1890-1910. A sudden surge in the demand for rubber causes the enslavement and brutal treatment of thousands of Indians.	
EVENTS IN NORTH AMERICA	Between 17,000-7,000 BC, the continents of Asia and America are linked by a land bridge- the Bering Straits. This is created by the fall in sea level caused by the last Ice Age.			Vitus Bering discovers Alaska in 1741. 1775-1783 American War of Independence	'Custer's Last Stand' in 1876. Sioux and Cheyenne Indians win Battle of Little Big Horn.	
EVENTS IN EUROPE	In the United Kingdom the ice sheet reaches as far south as the River Thames by 10,000 BC.	William of Normandy invaded England and became King in 1066.	In England Henry VIII is King from 1509-1547.	Mozart is born in 1756. French Revolution begins in 1789.	In 1889 Eiffel completed Tower in Paris. 1905 Einstein starts work on Theory of Relativity.	
EVENTS AROUND THE WORLD	Cave paintings in Australasia and Africa and stone axes in Australia in about 25,000 BC.	First Crusade started in 1096. From 1162-1227, Genghis Khan and the Mongol Hordes dominate eastern Europe and Asia.	In 1520 the explorer Magellan discovered the Straits into the Pacific Ocean from the Atlantic Ocean.	Captain Cook claims east coast of Australia for Britain in 1770. In 1789 the mutineers from HMS *Bounty* settled on Pitcairn Island in the Pacific Ocean.		

Girl with manioc

Marajo pot

1939-1945	1960s	1970-1979	1980-1989	1990s
Poor migrants from towns in north-eastern Brazil move into the Amazon to collect rubber for the 'war effort' as Japanese cut off supplies from the large plantations of Malaysia.	Xingu National Park created by the Villas-Boas brothers in central Brazil in 1961. In 1964, the Trans-Amazonian highway is started by military regime.	In 1976, the Trans-Amazonia road passed through the land of an uncontacted group of Parakana. Many died as a result of the contact.	In Altamira, Brazil, in 1989 Kayapo Indians organise international protest against huge dams. The Nahua Indians of Peru are contacted for the first time in 1984. Most die of Western diseases.	The United Nations declare 1993 'The Year of Indigenous Peoples'. A draft declaration of the rights of indigenous peoples (including Amazonian Indians) is under discussion at the UN.
1940 Walt Disney produced Fantasia. Attack on Pearl Harbour in 1941 brings USA into World War II.	In 1963, US President J.F. Kennedy is assassinated. In 1969, the Americans put the first man on the moon.			Bill Clinton is inaugurated as President of the USA in 1993.
Second World War breaks out Sept 1939.			Berlin Wall comes down in 1989.	Outbreak of civil war in Yugoslavia.
Rommel defeated by Montgomery at El Alamein in North Africa 1943. Atom bombs dropped on Hiroshima and Nagasaki in Japan in August 1945.		Population of China is over one billion by 1985.	Communist regimes collapse all over Europe.	

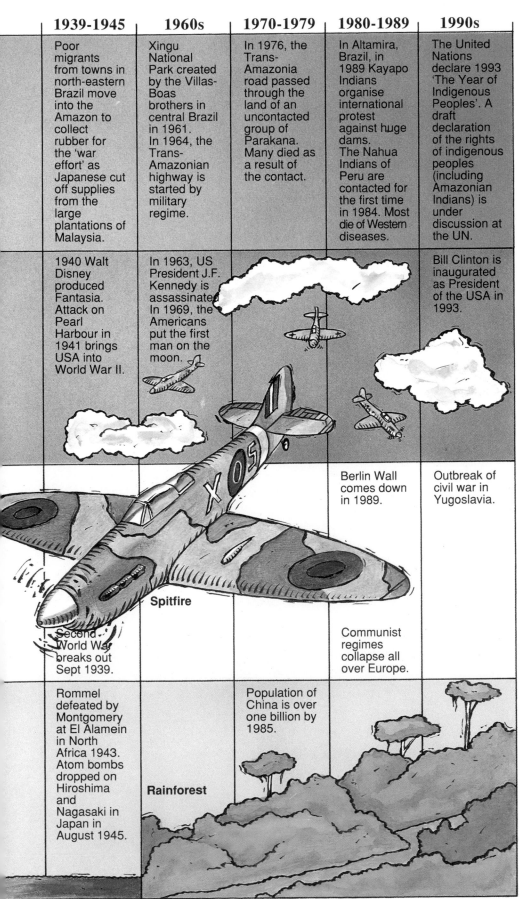

Spitfire

Rainforest

AMAZONIAN INDIAN HISTORY

The Amazonian Indians have been living in the rainforests of South America for at least 20,000 years. They continued to flourish during the rise and fall of the great Chinese, Greek and Roman empires. During this time they developed a way of life specially adapted to their rainforest environment in isolation from the rest of the world. It was only in 1498 when Christopher Columbus landed for the first time on the South American mainland that contact with the Western world began. Sadly smallpox and other diseases like measles and the common cold spread rapidly across the whole of South America killing a large proportion of the Indian population.

INTO THE FUTURE

Chief Aritana of the Yawalapiti tribe says, 'It is important that we never forget our traditions. I want our customs to last for ever and ever so that my son and his children will continue to live as we do'.

WHERE DO · THE · AMAZONIAN INDIANS GET THEIR · FOOD ? ·

The Amazon forest and grasslands have traditionally supplied Indians with all the food they need. Households generally make temporary gardens in the forest where they grow a great variety of vegetables, fruits and other plants. The staple crop for most Indians is manioc, a starchy tuber. Other important plants include maize, sweet potatoes, yams, peppers, pineapples and beans. Many kinds of palm fruit are collected from the forest as well as paw-paws, mangoes and avocados from garden plots. Much of the gardening is often women's work, while men hunt animals when they can. Tapirs, peccaries, pacas, agoutis, armadillos, monkeys and many kinds of bird are frequently caught, using bows and arrows, blowpipes and darts, and now shotguns. Fish and shellfish are caught in the rivers and streams.

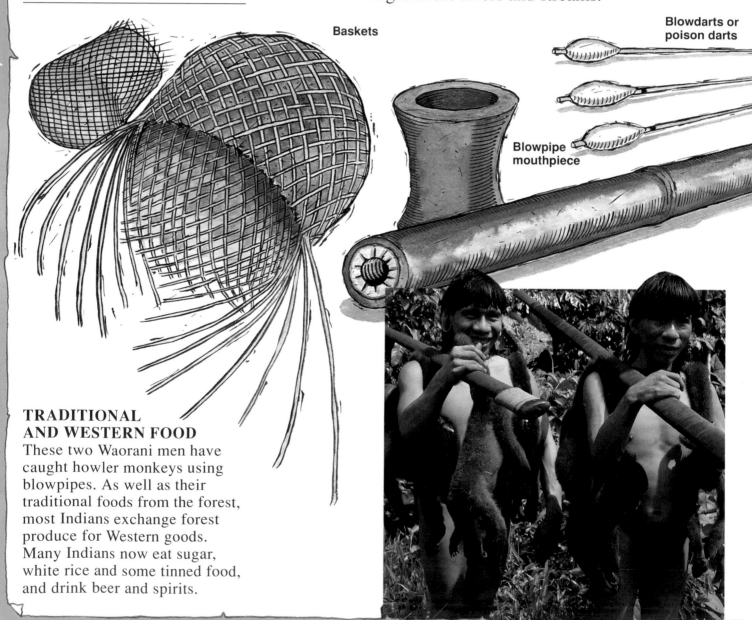

Baskets

Blowdarts or poison darts

Blowpipe mouthpiece

TRADITIONAL AND WESTERN FOOD

These two Waorani men have caught howler monkeys using blowpipes. As well as their traditional foods from the forest, most Indians exchange forest produce for Western goods. Many Indians now eat sugar, white rice and some tinned food, and drink beer and spirits.

MANIOC AND THE MOON

The Machiguenga live in south-eastern Peru. Like most other Indians their staple food is manioc. The long tubers are peeled and then boiled or toasted, and are also made into *masato*, a thirst-quenching drink. The Machiguenga believe that manioc was a gift to them from the moon, *Kashiri*. They say that long ago he came down from the sky in the form of a handsome man. At this time the Machiguenga say they just ate mud. *Kashiri* gave them cooked manioc tubers and showed them how to grow the plants. Because of this the Machiguenga believe that the plants are 'daughters' of the moon and must be cared for very well.

Blowpipe

FISHING

Fishing with bows and arrows is done by men and boys, but the whole family join in to fish with traps and poison from plants which stun the fish.

GARDENING

The picture above shows a group of Yanomami Indians gathering bananas from a forest plot. This is a family activity and everyone joins in. Though soils are often very poor, Indians are experts at cultivation and tend their gardens carefully. Many different crops are often grown together. After two or three years gardens are left to grow back into forest.

HUNTING

Indian men are skilful hunters but they are always careful not to catch too many animals. They know that they must conserve them for future generations. They also respect the creatures they hunt and ask their permission before they are killed. The Uru-Eu-Wau-Wau man on the left is hunting a peccary.

The traditional foods eaten by Amazonian Indians are very good indeed. The enormous range of fruit and vegetables grown, and the wild animals and fish available, provide well-balanced, nutritious meals. The amount of meat or fish eaten varies, but for almost all Indians, manioc (yuca or mandioca) is the staple food. The first meal of the day may be some manioc bread or some boiled or toasted manioc left over from the day before. A larger meal is eaten at mid-morning, this time with meat or fish if some has been caught. People eat snacks throughout the day: perhaps an avocado or mango, palm fruit or honey. A final meal is eaten after dark.

MANIOC BREAD
Some kinds of manioc have a poisonous juice inside them and after grating the tuber this must be squeezed out in a *tipiti*. Bread like this large, flat pancake below is then made from the toasted flour.

Tipiti

ABUNDANT FISH

Most Indians eat lots of fish. Amazonian rivers contain thousands of different kinds. This fish eats fruits that fall into the water. Indians hit their paddles on the water to attract the fish.

PALM FRUIT

The Indians make use of dozens of different palm trees. Many kinds, like *pataoa*, *jaci*, *bacaba* or *buriti* shown above, have delicious fruits that can be eaten cooked or raw or made into nourishing drinks. Many palm fruits are rich in oil which can be used for cooking when the fruits are crushed.

SHARING FOOD

Amazonian Indians believe that sharing food with others is one of the most important things they can do. To catch and then eat an animal all by yourself, for example, would be very bad manners. Similarly, garden work is shared as well as its produce. The Indian women above are helping each other to clear the ground for crops.

COOKING GAME

The Kayapo men here have been barbecuing peccary over an open fire. Game, like monkeys and birds, is often roasted on a spit. Sometimes a tortoise or armadillo is placed in the fire to cook. Some animals, such as deer and sloths, are not eaten because of their connections with the spirit world.

THE FOREST GARDEN

Indian families generally have two or three gardens in the forest. Each one may be about a hectare in size. Trees are felled then burned and crops are planted in between the charred logs. This protects the young plants from the sun and rain. One garden is often just for different kinds of manioc. But others will mix many crops like maize, peanuts, peppers, gourds, cotton and plants for medicines.

·DO THEY· ·HAVE· FAMILIES ·LIKE· ·OURS?·

Amazonian Indians live together in different kinds of family groups. But families generally have more members than just a mother, father and children. Grandparents, aunts, uncles and cousins can all live under the same roof. Some groups live in large communal houses where close family and relatives live together. Sometimes men can have more than one wife. Squabbles can break out, but normally people work together as a team. Looking after children is both men and women's work, so are collecting wild food and some fishing trips. But men and women often do different things. Men hunt, clear ground for gardens and make weapons. Women spin and weave cotton and prepare most food.

TEAM WORK

Children in Indian families don't have toys like ours. Most help their parents from an early age and this way they learn the skills they will need when they grow up and have families of their own. But they have a good time too! Young boys accompany their fathers on a hunt and the whole family will go on collecting trips in the forest, which can be good fun. Children help out in the gardens too. Their reward for this might be a tasty meal of sweet potatoes cooked where they were dug up. Sometimes someone finds a bees' nest and wild honey is eaten on the spot.

INTERMARRIAGE

In Brazil the families of some Amazonian Indian groups, like the Poyanawa on the left, include *caboclo* men and women. *Caboclos* are settlers who have lived in the forest for a very long time and who now live like Indians themselves. There are thousands of *caboclos* in Brazil.

 MARRIAGE

Among the tribes of the Amazon different rules for marriage exist. In some tribes a man may have more than one wife. But it is very rare for an Indian not to marry at all during his or her lifetime. Because Indians generally believe that they are reborn through their grandchildren, most want to have children. The Yanomami who live together in communal houses do not have a formal marriage ceremony but simply hang their hammocks next to each other.

NAMES

Traditionally Indians do not have first names or surnames. They use words that describe their relationship to each other like 'daughter' or 'my cousin'. But young children like this Waorani girl, are often given secret personal names before they are two years old. These are usually names of animals, flowers or birds.

TIME FOR CHILDREN

In most Indian families, babies and small children spend lots of time close at their mother's side. Yanomami Indians, below, pass the hottest hours of the day relaxing with their babies in cotton hammocks. Chief Aritana of the Yawalapiti says, 'We never hit children or even like to scold them. We like to pick them up and ask what is wrong because if we punish them they will grow up to be difficult and bad-tempered.'

·DO· AMAZONIAN INDIANS LIVE IN ·HOUSES?·

Amazonian Indians have traditionally lived in many different kinds of house. The most distinctive of these is the *maloca* or communal house. These are often immense, holding up to 150 people. Other Indians occupy much smaller single family houses that may be grouped together in a village or be spread out as isolated households in the forest or near a river. Houses are made from supporting poles, sometimes using tree bark panels. They are thatched with palm leaf fronds. Since missionaries started coming to the Amazon, Indian groups have become smaller so gradually, in many areas, fewer and fewer now live in communal houses.

THE COMMUNAL HOUSE

Communal houses, or *malocas*, take many varied forms, as Amazonian tribes have developed their own styles of architecture. Some may be oval, round or rectangular. They stay cool inside when it is hot, but are warm when the weather is cool. In the Xingu region, a typical *maloca* is 30-40 metres long and houses six to eight families. It serves as family home, workshop, meeting place, dance hall and temple. Some Yanomami groups live in a circle of individual shelters called a *shabono*. Each family has its own fire, with hammocks strung around it.

THE FAMILY HOUSE

The Quichua Indian house on the right is a single family dwelling. Like many others it is raised up on stilts to protect the family from the mud and rain and domestic animals. Many families now keep ducks or chickens and sometimes pigs. Inside, the family may sleep in hammocks or lie on the floor on sleeping mats. Planks cut from palm tree bark may be used for flooring or walls. Many houses are partially open-sided.

THE VILLAGE

The picture below shows a traditional Kayapo village. It has been built in the form of a circle, with one large house in the middle. Though men, women and children live in the cirlce of family houses, only the men use the central house. This is for meetings and ceremonies.

♪♭ LIVING TOGETHER ♪♭

Cooperation and sharing are very important parts of Indian life. Just as food is shared between relatives, so important activities like house-building are communal tasks. This is true of the construction of small family houses and giant *malocas*. In a communal house people cooperate in many different ways. Each woman makes her own manioc bread though meals are communal and served in the middle of the house. Everyone sits on the floor to eat as there are no tables or chairs. Communal houses have family compartments round the outside, where possessions are stored. Indians don't have beds, but sleep in hammocks or on mats on the floor.

PERSONAL POSSESSIONS

Waorani Indians keep all their personal possessions off the ground to keep them dry and away from insects. This includes the quivers of poisoned darts they use for hunting.

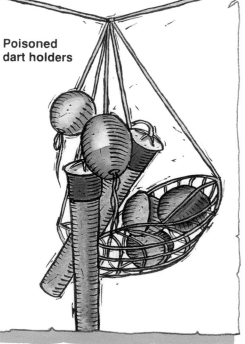

Poisoned dart holders

WHAT·DO AMAZONIAN ·INDIANS· ·WEAR?·

The hot and humid climate of the Amazon makes clothes largely unnecessary. It is traditional for Indians to wear very little at all except for ceremonial occasions. But some tribes like the Machiguenga and Ashaninka of Peru wear *cushmas* – long cotton garments like tunics – and the Yagua of eastern Peru once wore outfits that almost covered their bodies, made from *buriti* palm fibres. Men and women might wear leg and arm bands and necklaces, as well as cotton, bark cloth or beaded coverings. Ceremonial wear is usually very elaborate, with body paints, featherwork and body ornaments. Many Indians today wear some Western-style clothes.

WESTERN CLOTHING
The Waorani girl on the left is wearing a dress that she probably obtained from a missionary post near or in her village, or from a trader. Many Indians like to use their traditional body paint but wear Western clothes over the top, especially when outsiders visit them.

Necklace

PAST AND PRESENT
The Tsatchila Indian on the right is mixing traditional with modern dress. His distinctive helmet-like haircut is covered with red annatto paste. This ancient custom identifies his tribe. But the material over his shoulder and his bandana were bought from a store.

FIBRES FOR CLOTHES

Amazonian Indians use a variety of natural materials to make their everyday dress and ceremonial outfits. Feathers for head-dresses and beads, shells, animal teeth or iridescent beetle-wing cases for necklaces are held in place by homespun cotton, palm leaf or pineapple leaf cords. Plant fibres make fringed 'skirts' too, like those the Mehinaku are wearing on the right.

COLOUR WITH MESSAGES

The Suya man below is wearing red macaw feathers, black feathers, probably from a currasow, and yellow toucan feathers. Many Indians like this Suya man believe that yellow can connect them with the spirit world. Pet macaws are sometimes plucked and plant juices are rubbed onto their skin so that the new feathers grow back in a colour the Indians want.

PATTERNS WITH MEANING

The Kayapo, like most other tribes, paint their faces and bodies to show important things about themselves. Combinations of design and colour often show important stages in a person's life, like marriage. Patterns also show status at ceremonies or may help them to get in touch with the spirits.

RAINFOREST COLOUR

Different Amazonian tribes have developed a variety of distinguishing designs for their face and body painting. Most use the colours red and black. Both of these come from plants. The bright orange-red comes from seeds of the annatto tree or from the leaves of *Bignonia chica*; the black comes from genipapo fruit. The designs are usually applied with the fingers or a piece of cane. We also use the red colour from annatto seeds in our butter and margarine. Its trade name is E160(b).

· DO · AMAZONIAN INDIANS GO TO WORK ?

All Amazonian Indians work hard to obtain their food, build their homes and raise their families. Traditionally, men have hunted animals and done garden work for at least part of the day, while women have harvested crops like manioc, fetched water and prepared and cooked most of the food. Constructing houses and making implements also takes considerable time and effort. Since the arrival of Europeans, thousands of Indians have been forced to work for others, usually for nothing or for small sums of money. Today, many work as timber cutters on large estates that were once Indian lands, or as labourers in towns. The leaders of Amazonian Indian groups are working hard to improve this situation.

PORTABLE LIVES
Amazonian Indians are mostly nomadic – that is they do not live in any one place for long. This means that they need to be able to make everything they need from baskets like these to houses. It is hard work to build a new house from scratch.

Food baskets

WORK FOR THE SPIRITS
Traditional Indians do not distinguish between work and spare time. This Kreen-Akrore is making a head-dress. For him it is not a leisure activity, but part of what is necessary to be a Kreen-Akrore. The feathers have a special significance for the spirit world which the Indians believe controls their lives.

House-building for Amazonian Indians is a man's task. It is hard work and requires much expertise. First the ground must be cleared and then a plan may be traced out using vines to measure the proportions. Vines are also used to tie the main timbers together which have been cut from the forest using axes. The placing of cross beams and posts requires strength and skill. Houses are generally roofed with palm leaves or bunches of grass from savannah areas. There is usually a celebration when a house is completed.

TIMES OF SLAVERY

Since the sixteenth century the Indian peoples of South America have been treated by many as slaves. The picture above shows chained Indians, forced to collect rubber during the 'rubber boom', which lasted until 1911. Thousands died working to provide rubber for the European car tyre industry.

SELLING CULTURE

The picture to the left shows Kofan Indians selling necklaces. Oil and agricultural projects have disrupted their traditional way of life so they sell artifacts to make money for food and Western goods.

WORKING TO DEFEND TERRITORY

Davi Yanomami above and many other Indians now have to work hard to protect their traditional lands. He talks at conferences, gives TV interviews and generally helps represent the views of the Yanomami Indians to outsiders.

WOOD AND WATER

Two of the more arduous chores in a typical Amazonian Indian's day are collecting wood for fires and water to drink. These tasks are carried out mainly by women and children.

WHAT DO AMAZONIAN INDIANS DO ·IN THEIR· SPARE TIME?

Spare time as we know it would be a puzzle to most Amazonian Indians. What we divide into work and recreational activities are to them linked together and are as important as each other. Time not spent in hunting or preparing food, for example, is often used for making useful implements, playing with children or telling myths or stories. All have their place in the normal activities that ensure the day-to-day well-being of each group. Some tribes take part in ritual contests and games (such as wrestling) and mark important ceremonies with celebrations that can last for many days.

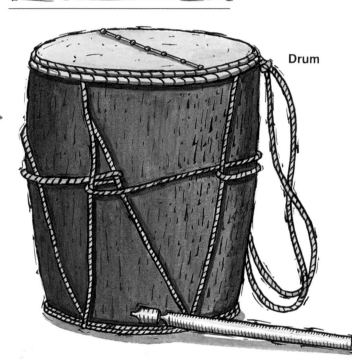

Drum

MAKING IMPLEMENTS
While resting, the Waorani man below is weaving a basket from cane. This is one of the many things Indian men make.

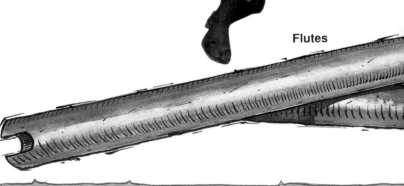

Flutes

TESTS OF STRENGTH

In the Xingu National Park friendly wrestling matches take place between the men of different tribes after the *moitara*. This is the occasion when goods are bartered or exchanged. Here, two Mehinaku men are competing. Similar strength tests are performed by the Tukano in Colombia.

BATHING

Bathing is enjoyed by men, women and children alike. Indians are very conscious of cleanliness and believe the body should be looked after well. Soon after dawn people go down to their nearest river to bathe. Indians don't need to use soap or towels like we do.

FESTIVAL DANCING

Traditional tribes have various festivals and ceremonies during the year. These might be to celebrate harvests. It is common for Indians to sing, play instruments and dance like the Kayapo on the left.

Shuttlecock

MUSICAL INSTRUMENTS

Indians enjoy music, but it has a cultural meaning too. The Yawalapiti men above are playing sacred flutes. Men might play bamboo panpipes or flutes made of animal bone as well as drums.

DO BOYS AND GIRLS ·GO TO· ·SCHOOL?·

Traditional Amazonian Indian communities have never needed to send boys and girls to school. Instead, children have learnt useful skills by watching and helping their parents in almost everything they do. Missionaries first introduced schools to Indian children in an attempt to convert them to Christianity and in recent years some governments have started education programmes. Many Indian groups now have schools, and children learn maths, Western history and how to read and write in Spanish or Portuguese. Unfortunately, what they are taught often is not useful to them in their way of life.

LEARNING FOR LIFE
By the age of twelve or thirteen a typical Indian boy is very capable and knows what he wants to do in life. Having watched and shared in every adult activity from late childhood, he will soon have learned most of the things he needs to know. This Matses boy is already a fine fisherman.

FITNESS IN THE FOREST
Fitness and agility are important to Amazonian Indians. These Achuar children are not only enjoying themselves but are developing the agility and balance necessary for later life. Hunting, gardening, fetching water and many other activities require strength and fitness.

THE ART OF LIVING
The Juruna girl below is learning from her mother how to make a pot. The pot is not considered to be a real one until the final decoration is complete. This is because, to the Indians, the way something is made cannot be separated from what it is used for.

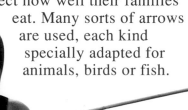 **LANGUAGES**

Each Amazonian tribe has its own language, and the three largest groups of language are Arawak, Carib and Tupi-Guarani. Members of tribes can often speak the language of their neighbours as well as Spanish or Portuguese. In some tribes the men and women speak a different form of the same language. Some of the words we use come from Indian languages, for example jaguar comes from the Guarani word *jaguá*.

SKILLS TO SURVIVE
The Yanomami boys below are practising with their fathers' bows and arrows. They need to practise to develop the skills that they will need to feed their own families. Their skills will affect how well their families eat. Many sorts of arrows are used, each kind specially adapted for animals, birds or fish.

FOREIGN TEACHING
The school above is typical of those found all over Amazonia. The Indians and *caboclo* (settler) children here are being taught Portuguese. Government teachers or missionaries learn just enough of an Indian language to speak to the children. The school teaches children of different ages all together. School starts very early in the morning until midday.

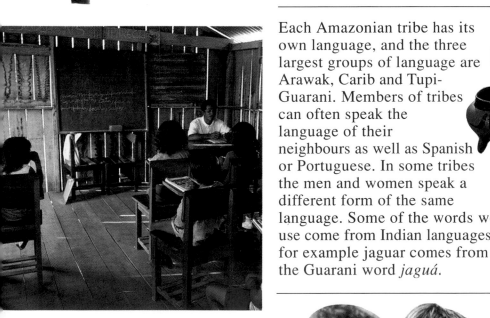

·ARE THE· AMAZONIAN INDIANS ·ARTISTS?·

Amazonian Indians do not think that art or artistic ability is different from the wide variety of skills needed for everyday life. For them, each object has a very definite form and special use. For example, they may not think a pot exists until every detail or decoration is complete. This even includes the design on the bottom which will be blackened on its first use on an open fire. To Indians the beauty and value of an object generally depends on how useful it is. A useless object therefore is not seen as being beautiful. Colour and patterns are extremely important to Amazonian Indians.

ANIMAL SPIRITS
The stylised drawings here were made by Indians of the Xingu region in Brazil. They represent creatures which are important in their everyday life and in the spirit world, like the dangerous anaconda.

Turtle

Stork

Caiman

Ray

Piranha

Anaconda

SHIPIBO POTTERY
The Shipibo Indians of Peru have produced some of the finest pottery in Amazonia. The pattern of lines on this pot is painted with different coloured earth.

PATTERNS WITH MEANING

To outsiders, the striking patterns and designs made by Amazonians Indians are often seen as being beautiful, but that's all. But the Xingu designs of birds and animals, for example, represent creatures important in the spirit world. The complex geometrical patterns on artifacts like the Marajo pot illustrated on the right can represent the invisible aspects of Indian lives, such as their view of the universe. Designs that are repeated or symmetrical can represent stability and also mark a tribe's identity.

Marajo pot

ART WITH PURPOSE
The sieve on the right is for straining palm fruit juice. It is cleverly designed with a regular pattern of criss-crossing palm fibres. It is both useful and beautiful.

USEFUL PALMS
Amazonian Indians are particularly skilful at using materials from the forest. Below, a Kayapo is making a basket from palm leaves. Fibres from palms are very useful.

Sieve

BARASANA PAINTING
Above, a Barasana man is painting the front of his *maloca*, or house. Designs are made in chalk, ochre and charcoal representing dancers, spirits and visions.

Amazonian Indians did not traditionally write books. They did not have an alphabet like ours or use paper of any kind. Most did, however, develop drawings and special symbols representing animals, birds and the spirit world that were worked into baskets or drawn on cloth, pottery or the face and body. Some made petroglyphs or rock carvings. Today, the representatives of Indian groups work in offices and write long reports describing their history and demands.

shima

THE CHRONICLERS' RECORDS

Numerous books and accounts of Indian life were written by Spanish and Portuguese chroniclers in the sixteenth and seventeenth centuries. Because Indian society was so different from theirs they often gave very misleading accounts and described the Indians as savages. Today, some Indians like this Kayapo are recording important events for themselves.

atawa

tsorito

INDIAN LANGUAGE

For most Indian tribes, missionaries were the first to try and write down their languages. Today, some Indians can write in their own languages. These words are in Machiguenga.

matsontsori

Knowledge and beliefs have always been passed down by word of mouth in Indian societies and this tradition still exists today. Complicated myths or stories involving animals and other creatures of the rainforest, as well as cosmic beings like the sun and moon, are told or sung. Children memorise these songs or stories from an early age. The Taruma Indians of Guyana, for example, believe that the father of the first woman was a giant anaconda and that the seeds of all the edible fruits and plants fell out from inside his tail when it was cut off.

DESIGN AND MEANING

The symbols below were made by Indians long ago, whose territory is now the Brazilian state of Amazonas. All these designs, carved into rock, conveyed important messages and probably related to the spirit world. Today, no one knows exactly what they mean.

POLITICAL MESSAGES

The sign behind the people seated above is written in Spanish. It says: 'Eleventh Annual Meeting of the Coordinating Body of the Indigenous Organisations of the Amazon Basin.' The representative at this meeting seated in the middle can write in Aguaruna and Spanish.

PETROGLYPHS

The boulder on the right is one of several carved rocks called petroglyphs found in south-east Peru. Local Machiguenga Indians say that they do not know what these ancient signs mean but believe the rocks are the 'houses' of spirits.

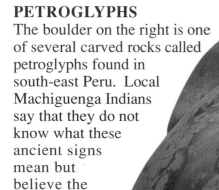

· D O · AMAZONIAN INDIANS GO · TO THE · DOCTOR ?

Most Amazonian Indians have some knowledge of healing and mainly use plants as medicines. One person, however, has special skills in identifying and curing illnesses. This is the shaman. By putting himself in touch with the spirit world, he can find and remove the cause of illness. This is often thought to be a substance or object put there by an evil shaman. The shaman smokes or takes drugs which give him visions and help him to make contact with the spirit world. The arrival of Europeans in South America brought to the Indians a whole new range of diseases, most of which they cannot cure themselves. Very few Indians have been treated with Western medicines and many are still dying today from illnesses like 'flu and measles.

PLANTS THAT HEAL

The Amazonian Indians have known about and used the healing powers of rainforest plants for a very long time. The Kayapo tribe, for instance, are familiar with around 650 medicinal plants.

Medicinal plant

The Indians' knowledge is being lost as the size of their groups and territories is reduced because of contact with outsiders. The bushy plant shown here has lemon-flavoured leaves which help cure fevers. The monkey-tail vine on the left is used for upset stomachs.

FATAL CONTACT

There were once over 2,000 Uru-Eu-Wau-Wau Indians (below). They were contacted for the first time recently. Since then half have died from Western diseases.

32

A number of rainforest plants used by Amazonian Indians are now helping people all round the world to get well. One example is an ingredient of the arrow poison *curare*. This is now widely used in Western medicine to make muscles relax. Many different sorts of *curare* are made by Indians, especially in the north-west Amazon. For instance, the Kofan Indians of Colombia make *curare* from a forest fruit. But the best known ingredients come from two kinds of vine. A chemical called *tubocurarine* is obtained from them and used for illnesses such as tetanus and multiple sclerosis, and for eye surgery.

A CURE FOR MALARIA

The bark of these young *Cinchona* trees contains quinine which we use to treat malaria. Ecuadorian and Peruvian Indians were the first to use the bark.

BARK MEDICINES

The bark of vines or trees contains high concentrations of chemicals. Indians like this Kayapo man above have discovered that these chemicals can make powerful medicines.

VACCINATIONS

This Uru-Eu-Wau-Wau child is lucky. He is being vaccinated at a Brazilian Indian Agency post to help protect him from the diseases brought in by outsiders. Half of his tribe died from just one disease – malaria. Indians only rarely receive Western medicines.

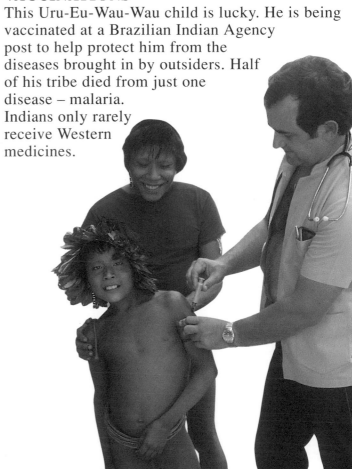

· D O T H E ·
AMAZONIAN
I N D I A N S
BELIEVE IN
LIFE AFTER
· D E A T H ? ·

Amazonian Indians believe that after death the soul leaves the body and joins the spirit world. The spirits of the dead – a person's ancestors – inhabit a special region either above or below the surface of the earth. Most groups believe in a universe that has many different levels or layers. These are occupied by different kinds of spirit being, both good and evil. The souls of the dead can come to visit the living on earth, especially if they are unhappy. Amongst traditional Indian groups, a dead person is sometimes buried in the forest or at the site of his or her home. From here they will begin their long journey to the after-life by boat.

SNUFF
The taking of snuff to bring on visions is an important ritual for men in most tribes. Many plants have this effect and the visions put men in touch with the spirits in the plants, trees, rocks and streams of the forest as well as the souls of the dead. The Yanomami man on the left is preparing a plant snuff.

POSTS OF THE DEAD
When an Indian dies he is buried with his private belongings. For a woman this may be pottery or a basket; for a man, bows and arrows and perhaps a snuff holder. Sometimes a bow and arrow is placed on the grave, as weapons may be needed for the dangerous journey to the place where the dead will live on. The man on the right is decorating the 'Posts of the Dead' in his village. The designs are to protect the people from evil spirits who may wish to return.

PIPING AWAY THE SPRITS

The Xingu tribesmen on the left are performing a special ceremony. The girl has just ended some time in seclusion marking the end of her childhood. Using huge sacred bamboo flutes, the men are going from hut to hut piping away the bad spirits who may harm her.

THE KUARUP

Among the tribes of the Xingu region the special Kuarup ceremony is performed when an Indian of chiefly status dies. Songs and wrestling matches are part of the religious rites.

THE JAGUAR

Most Indian groups believe that a man's spirit can leave his body while he is asleep and go wandering in the forest. But because of his special powers, the shaman can take on the form of a jaguar at any time. To most Indians the jaguar, the most dangerous animal in the forest, has a special connection with the spirit world. In the form of a jaguar the shaman can visit the region where the spirits live.

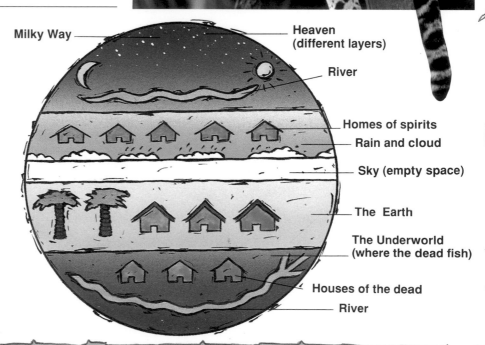

THE AFTERLIFE

The drawing on the right is a copy of a map drawn by a Machiguenga Indian. It represents the universe or cosmos as the Machiguenga Indians believe it to be. They say that when they die they travel from the earth to an underworld where their souls live on. Here they can carry on doing things they did when they were alive, like living in houses and fishing. The rivers on earth are thought to flow into a river in the underworld and into a special river that exists in heaven.

Milky Way

Heaven (different layers)

River

Homes of spirits

Rain and cloud

Sky (empty space)

The Earth

The Underworld (where the dead fish)

Houses of the dead

River

HOW DO THE AMAZONIAN INDIANS · TRAVEL? ·

In Amazonia, the rivers are the highways and canoes are the best form of transport. Indian groups do not often stay in one place for long. Animals are also often hunted far from home. Households or whole villages will move to find new areas for hunting and gardening, or sometimes following a death. Their traditional way of cultivating areas of the forest for food means that they move their gardens often so that the land is not exhausted. They can travel a long way in order to hunt. Short journeys are generally made on foot. Indians make a network of narrow paths through the forest, connecting houses with gardens and hunting grounds.

Girl carrying manioc

ROADS
The governments of Amazonian countries see roads as a sign of progress and many pass through regions once only accessible by canoe. Most roads cut through Indian lands – the one above cuts through Waimiri-Atroari territory – but instead of helping the Indians, roads have brought thousands of settlers who claim their lands.

MAKING CANOES

The building of a log canoe is an important activity for men and boys and requires great expertise. Some canoes are made from a single sheet of bark. This is done by peeling the bark off a log in one piece after a long slit has been made down one side. Wooden cross-members are then inserted. Tucks made at each end and on each side will bring the ends up above the water line. 'Dug-out' canoes are made from a single trunk, hollowed out and shaped using a hoe-like blade, then widened and strengthened by burning.

TRAVEL BY PLANE

Indians rarely travel by plane. Most planes that land in Indian territory carry missionaries, gold miners or anthropologists. Indians, like some of the Yanomami, have been flown to makeshift hospitals, but few can afford to buy the very expensive petrol.

SKILL ON WATER

Amazonian rivers like the Jurua, above, rise by as much as 6-10 metres during the rains, making them dangerous. But most Indians are skilful oarsmen.

THE NAHUA

Travel by canoe is the only form of transport the Nahua of Peru and most Indians have ever known. This group are taking the embers of their fire to a new house as fire is very precious to them.

DO·THE AMAZONIAN INDIANS HAVE RULERS?

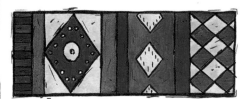

Amazonian Indians do not have rulers in the way we do. Living in small groups makes them unnecessary. Any authority is held by the head of a household or family group. Within these groups though, the shaman occupies a position of prestige because of his links with the spirits. He may guide the rest of the group by discussion. Today, some larger groups have chiefs who make decisions that influence everyone. All groups are also subject to the laws of the countries they happen to live in.

INDIAN CHIEFS

The term 'chief' or 'headman' which to us signifies power, means something very different to Amazonian peoples. In many groups the headman is responsible for the well-being of the household. He also oversees the community activities such as building a new communal house. His most important role, however, is as a link between the shaman and the community. He does not punish, command or issue orders but advises and helps keep tribal harmony. Below is Davi Yanomami who is a local Yanomami chief and he also represents them around the world.

In every Indian community the shaman is regarded with great respect because he has special powers. From an early age he is trained to be able to communicate with the spirit world at all times. He can do this by taking substances made from plants that give him visions. These allow him to find out why an illness has been caused, and then cure it. The shaman also knows more myths than anybody else and the real meaning behind them. Smoking is another way the shaman brings on a state of trance to contact the spirits. He also guides his community through important rituals.

THE KAYAPO MEN'S HOUSE

The men's house is a place where the head of each household comes to discuss problems and reach decisions. Above, Kayapo men discuss an issue which affects their people. No one person has the power to force his decisions on everyone else.

COLUMBUS

In 1498, Christopher Columbus landed on the mainland of South America. He was trying to discover a new sea route to the East Indies. He claimed the land for Spain, whom he believed had the right to rule this new land.

·DO THE· AMAZONIAN ·INDIANS· HAVE ARMIES?

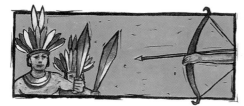

When Europeans first arrived in Amazonia, warfare between tribes was carried out for a number of reasons. It was not usually carried out to claim territory, however, but to avenge wrongs that might be real or imagined. Some tribes practised war as a sport, or to prove the prestige of warriors. War was also made to capture prisoners as slaves, or to take trophies. The Jivaro of Ecuador are famous for making shrunken heads from their enemies. Some tribes assembled huge warring parties involving hundreds of men. Warfare between tribes no longer happens today. Recently Indians have been engaged in a war of words to try to save their traditional way of life.

WEAPONS AND WARRIORS

The weapons of war were the club, bow and arrow and spear. Sometimes the arrows were tipped with poison. This Kayapo warrior is painted and decorated as if ready for a battle. This is very important as it marks which tribe he belongs to and makes him more intimidating. He was protesting at Altamira in 1989.

TRADITIONAL WEAPONS

In the past some tribes used carefully decorated war clubs made of wood. Shields were made of wood or animal skins. Spears were up to 2 metres long and arrows were often tipped with bone heads.

Bow and arrow

ATAHUALPA

Amazonian Indians have resisted hostile invasions by Westerners throughout their history. In 1742, for example, Juan Santos Atahualpa brought together the Yanesha and Ashaninka tribes of Peru. They defended the Peruvian Amazon from colonisation for over 100 years.

ALTAMIRA

The photograph on the left was taken at a rally organised by the Kayapo Indians in 1989 at Altamira in Brazil. Over 500 Indians attended demanding a halt to plans for dams that would flood their ancestral lands. The Altamira conference (below) gained international publicity resulting in the World Bank withdrawing finance for the dam project. The decision was a major victory for the Indians and gained much sympathy for their cause.

Spear

WARRIOR WOMEN

The first expedition down the Amazon river was led by Francisco de Orellana in 1542. During this voyage Orellana was told about a tribe of fierce warrior women. These women were said to attack villages to capture husbands. They were called 'Amazons' by explorers as this was the word the ancient Greeks had used for a legendary nation of female warriors in Asia. No evidence has ever been found that they really existed!

· WHAT IS · HAPPENING · TO THE · AMAZONIAN INDIANS ?

Amazonian Indians were the first people to live in the rainforest. They have used it, without destroying it, for thousands of years and so have a right to live there now. This is what most Indians want today. But for the last 500 years they have been victims of the intolerance and greed of the more powerful society around them. Governments do not want to officially acknowledge Indian lands and have encouraged people from other parts of the country to colonise them. Road building, ranching, logging, large-scale agriculture, dams, oil prospecting, tourism, missionaries and military projects are seriously threatening the well-being of Indians today. But Indians are trying to defend their rights and represent themselves when important decisions are made.

GOLD MINING

In 1989, about 45,000 gold miners – *garimpeiros* – invaded the lands of the 9,000 Yanomami who live in north-eastern Brazil. The effect on the Indians was disastrous. About 1,500 died from diseases the miners introduced and enormous environmental damage was done. The *garimpeiros* attacked riverbeds and banks with high-pressure jets of water, destroying them completely. They also poisoned rivers with mercury and shot many wild animals. Many miners are still refusing to leave the area even though the government has told them to go.

SPEAKING OUT

Above, Raoni, a Kayapo chief is interviewed on the radio about the problems the Kayapo and other Indians have had defending their lands. Settlers have destroyed large areas of trees, and dams threaten their lifestyle even more.

THE WAY FORWARD
Indians like Paulinho Paiakan below are insisting that their demands about their lands are respected. They have developed plans to protect their way of life and the Amazon rainforest itself.

DISAPPEARING FOREST
About ten per cent of Amazonian rainforest has already disappeared. Most of it has been burned by wealthy businessmen who try to claim the land for themselves. In this way much land has been taken from Amazonian Indians and serious ecological problems have been caused.

ALL IN THE SAME BOAT

Ailton Krenak is one of the Indians determined to stop the rainforest from being destroyed. He has said: 'We have lived in this place for a long time, a very long time, since the time when the world did not yet have this shape. We learned with the ancients that we are a tiny part of this immense universe, fellow travellers with all the animals, the plants and the waters. We are all a part of the whole, we cannot neglect or destroy our home. And now we want to talk to those who cannot yet manage to see the world in this way, to say to them that together we have to take care of the boat in which we are all sailing.'

· GLOSSARY ·

AMAZONIA The region of South America through which the Amazon river and its tributaries flow.

ARCHITECTURE The design and construction of buildings.

ANTHROPOLOGIST Someone who studies how other people live.

ARTEFACT An object made by people.

BARTER To exchange goods without using money.

COLONISE To move into an area in order to settle there.

COMMUNAL Shared with other people.

COSMIC Relating to the universe.

CABOCLOS Descendant of a marriage between an Amazonian Indian and a settler.

ECOLOGY The way natural things relate to each other and their surroundings.

ENVIRONMENT Our surroundings, including the land, rivers, oceans and the air.

FIBRES Fine, stringy threads found in plant stems and leaves which can be woven or spun together.

GAME Wild animals hunted for food.

GARIMPEIROS A miner or prospector.

GOURD Hollow, hard skin of the fruit of the calabash tree. It is used by the Indians as a bowl or water container.

HALLUCINOGENIC Causing visions or dreams.

IRIDESCENT Rainbow-like, gleaming colours.

MALOCA A large Amazonian Indian house, big enough for several families to live in.

MANIOC A root vegetable that looks like a long potato. There are many different kinds.

MERCURY An extremely poisonous, silvery white heavy metal that is liquid at room temperature.

MIGRATION Moving into new areas to live.

MISSIONARIES Members of a Christian religion who travel to other parts of the world to persuade other peoples to become Christians.

MYTH A traditional story about magical beings.

PECCARY A large pig-like animal hunted by the Indians for food.

RAINFOREST Dense forest with heavy rainfall found in tropical areas.

RITUAL Traditional ceremony or actions performed in the same way each time.

SAVANNAH A large area of open grassland with occasional trees, found in hot countries.

SNUFF Powdered tobacco or other hallucinogenic plant leaves taken by sniffing it up the nose.

SHAMAN A witch-doctor who has special contact with the spirit world.

STAPLE Main type of food eaten.

TIPITI A long tube made of basketware used for squeezing the poisonous juice out of some kinds of manioc.

TRIBUTARY A river or stream flowing into a larger river or lake.

TUBER A swollen underground part of a plant. Potatoes are tubers.

♦ INDEX ♦